Henri Cartier-Bresson, Paris, 1958.
Copyright © Henri Cartier-Bresson/Magnum Photos, Inc., New York.
From the TINY FOLIO™ *Hugs & Kisses,* available from Abbeville Press

Place stamp here

ABBEVILLE PUBLISHING GROUP
22 Cortlandt Street · New York, N.Y. 10007

Gilles Peress, 1973.
From the TINY FOLIO™ *Hugs & Kisses,* available from Abbeville Press

ABBEVILLE PUBLISHING GROUP
22 Cortlandt Street · New York, N.Y. 10007

Elliott Erwitt, Paris, 1970.
Copyright © Elliott Erwitt/Magnum Photos, Inc., New York.
From the Tiny Folio™ *Hugs & Kisses,* available from Abbeville Press

ABBEVILLE PUBLISHING GROUP
22 Cortlandt Street · New York, N.Y. 10007

Marc Riboud, 1953.

From the TINY FOLIO™ *Hugs & Kisses,* available from Abbeville Press

ABBEVILLE PUBLISHING GROUP
22 Cortlandt Street · New York, N.Y. 10007

Thomas Hoepker, New York, 1990.
Copyright © Thomas Hoepker/Magnum Photos, Inc,. New York.
From the TINY FOLIO™ *Hugs & Kisses,* available from Abbeville Press

Place stamp here

ABBEVILLE PUBLISHING GROUP
22 Cortlandt Street · New York, N.Y. 10007

Eliott Erwitt, 1962.

Copyright © Elliott Erwitt/Magnum Photos, Inc., New York.

From the TINY FOLIO™ *Hugs & Kisses,* available from Abbeville Press

Place stamp here

ABBEVILLE PUBLISHING GROUP
22 Cortlandt Street · New York, N.Y. 10007

Eric Kroll, Canton, China, 1990.
Copyright © Eric Kroll/Omni-Photo Communications, Inc., New York.
From the Tiny Folio™ *Hugs & Kisses,* available from Abbeville Press

Place stamp here

ABBEVILLE PUBLISHING GROUP
22 Cortlandt Street · New York, N.Y. 10007

Burt Glinn, Fire Island, New York, 1961.
Copyright © Burt Glinn/Magnum Photos, Inc., New York.
From the TINY FOLIO™ *Hugs & Kisses,* available from Abbeville Press

Place stamp here

ABBEVILLE PUBLISHING GROUP
22 Cortlandt Street · New York, N.Y. 10007

P. J. Griffiths, date unknown.

Copyright © P. J. Griffiths/Magnum Photos, Inc., New York.

From the Tiny Folio™ *Hugs & Kisses,* available from Abbeville Press

ABBEVILLE PUBLISHING GROUP

22 Cortlandt Street · New York, N.Y. 10007

Dennis Stock, Paris, 1958.
Copyright © Dennis Stock/Magnum Photos, Inc., New York.
From the TINY FOLIO™ *Hugs & Kisses,* available from Abbeville Press

Place stamp here

ABBEVILLE PUBLISHING GROUP
22 Cortlandt Street · New York, N.Y. 10007

Henri Cartier-Bresson, Paris, 1969.
Copyright © Henri Cartier-Bresson/Magnum Photos, Inc., New York.
From the TINY FOLIO™ *Hugs & Kisses,* available from Abbeville Press

Place stamp here

ABBEVILLE PUBLISHING GROUP
22 Cortlandt Street · New York, N.Y. 10007

Bruce Davidson, New York, 1960.
Copyright © Bruce Davidson/Magnum Photos, Inc., New York.
From the TINY FOLIO™ *Hugs & Kisses,* available from Abbeville Press

Place stamp here

ABBEVILLE PUBLISHING GROUP
22 Cortlandt Street · New York, N.Y. 10007

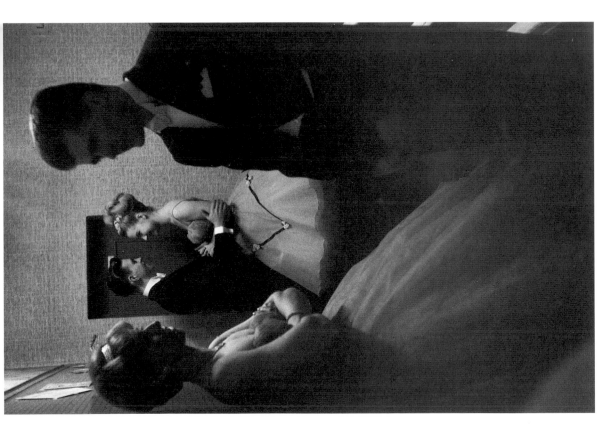

David Hurn, date unknown.
Copyright © David Hurn/Magnum Photos, Inc., New York.
From the TINY FOLIO™ *Hugs & Kisses*, available from Abbeville Press

Place stamp here

ABBEVILLE PUBLISHING GROUP
22 Cortlandt Street · New York, N.Y. 10007

Elliott Erwitt, California, 1955.
Copyright © Elliott Erwitt/Magnum Photos, Inc., New York.
From the TINY FOLIO™ *Hugs & Kisses*, available from Abbeville Press

ABBEVILLE PUBLISHING GROUP
22 Cortlandt Street · New York, N.Y. 10007

Ernst Haas, New York, 1958.
Copyright © Ernst Haas/Magnum Photos, Inc., New York.
From the Tiny Folio™ *Hugs & Kisses,* available from Abbeville Press

Place stamp here

ABBEVILLE PUBLISHING GROUP
22 Cortlandt Street · New York, N.Y. 10007

Elliott Erwitt, Valencia, Spain, 1952.
Copyright © Elliott Erwitt/Magnum Photos, Inc., New York.
From the TINY FOLIO™ *Hugs & Kisses,* available from Abbeville Press

Place stamp here

ABBEVILLE PUBLISHING GROUP
22 Cortlandt Street · New York, N.Y. 10007

Henry Cartier-Bresson, Dieppe, France, 1929.
Copyright © Henri Cartier-Bresson/Magnum Photos, Inc., New York.
From the TINY FOLIO™ *Hugs & Kisses,* available from Abbeville Press

Place stamp here

ABBEVILLE PUBLISHING GROUP
22 Cortlandt Street · New York, N.Y. 10007

Bruce Davidson, New York, 1959.
Copyright © Bruce Davidson/Magnum Photos, Inc., New York.
From the TINY FOLIO™ *Hugs & Kisses,* available from Abbeville Press

Place stamp here

ABBEVILLE PUBLISHING GROUP
22 Cortlandt Street · New York, N.Y. 10007

Franco Zecchin, Palermo, Italy, 1987.
Copyright © Franco Zecchin/Magnum Photos, Inc., New York.
From the Tiny Folio™ *Hugs & Kisses,* available from Abbeville Press

Place stamp here

ABBEVILLE PUBLISHING GROUP
22 Cortlandt Street · New York, N.Y. 10007

Elliott Erwitt, date unknown.

From the TINY FOLIO™ *Hugs & Kisses,* available from Abbeville Press

Place stamp here

ABBEVILLE PUBLISHING GROUP
22 Cortlandt Street · New York, N.Y. 10007

Elliott Erwitt, New York, 1955.
Copyright © Elliott Erwitt/Magnum Photos, Inc., New York.
From the TINY FOLIO™ *Hugs & Kisses,* available from Abbeville Press

Place stamp here

ABBEVILLE PUBLISHING GROUP
22 Cortlandt Street · New York, N.Y. 10007

Elliott Erwitt, Kraków, Poland, 1964.
Copyright © Elliott Erwitt/Magnum Photos, Inc., New York.
From the TINY FOLIO™ *Hugs & Kisses,* available from Abbeville Press

ABBEVILLE PUBLISHING GROUP
22 Cortlandt Street · New York, N.Y. 10007

Richard Kalvar, New York, date unknown.
Copyright © Richard Kalvar/Magnum Photos, Inc., New York.
From the TINY FOLIO™ *Hugs & Kisses,* available from Abbeville Press

Place stamp here

ABBEVILLE PUBLISHING GROUP
22 Cortlandt Street · New York, N.Y. 10007

Danny Lyon, 1985.
Copyright © Danny Lyon/Magnum Photos, Inc., New York.
From the TINY FOLIO™ *Hugs & Kisses,* available from Abbeville Press

ABBEVILLE PUBLISHING GROUP
22 Cortlandt Street · New York, N.Y. 10007

Leonard Freed, New York, 1963.

From the TINY FOLIO™ *Hugs & Kisses,* available from Abbeville Press

Place stamp here

ABBEVILLE PUBLISHING GROUP
22 Cortlandt Street · New York, N.Y. 10007

Place stamp here

Mark J. Goebel, 1993.
Copyright © Mark J. Goebel/Omni-Photo Communications, Inc., New York.
From the Tiny Folio™ *Hugs & Kisses,* available from Abbeville Press

ABBEVILLE PUBLISHING GROUP
22 Cortlandt Street · New York, N.Y. 10007

Richard Kalvar, Paris, 1965.
Copyright © Richard Kalvar/Magnum Photos, Inc., New York.
From the Tiny Folio™ *Hugs & Kisses,* available from Abbeville Press

Place stamp here

ABBEVILLE PUBLISHING GROUP
22 Cortlandt Street · New York, N.Y. 10007

Elliott Erwitt, date unknown.

From the Tiny Folio™ *Hugs & Kisses,* available from Abbeville Press

ABBEVILLE PUBLISHING GROUP
22 Cortlandt Street · New York, N.Y. 10007

Sonja Bullaty, c. 1950s.
Copyright © Sonja Bullaty, New York.
From the TINY FOLIO™ *Hugs & Kisses,* available from Abbeville Press

Place stamp here

ABBEVILLE PUBLISHING GROUP
22 Cortlandt Street · New York, N.Y. 10007

J. K., near Naples, Italy, date unknown.
Copyright © J. K./Magnum Photos, Inc., New York.
From the TINY FOLIO™ *Hugs & Kisses,* available from Abbeville Press

Copyright © 1998 Abbeville Press, Inc. Printed in Hong Kong.

ABBEVILLE PUBLISHING GROUP
22 Cortlandt Street · New York, N.Y. 10007